Send an email to johnballis@leanyourway.com with the subject line, "Lean to Cash," and get a ROI spreadsheet to help identify areas where you can save money. After that, we can schedule a meeting to discuss it further.

Endorsements

"John Ballis was a founder of George Group consulting and led some of our earliest deployments and wins of Lean Six sigma. His new book on Rapid ROI is an important and logical 'next step' in continuous improvement, which I recommend."
Michael George
Former CEO, George Group Consultants

"John is one of those rare Lean consultants who know how to get long-term results. You will enjoy reading his book on Rapid ROI and working with him. I highly recommend this for all leaders committed to learning how to execute change for lasting results."
Norman Bodek
Owner PCS Pres—Godfather of Lean

"John Ballis, often referred to as the Master of Continuous Improvement, has a new book, Rapid ROI, that is a must-read for all CEOs. Focusing on Continuous Improvement via an engaged culture that flows throughout your entire organization and results in immediate waste reduction, John provides a simple but powerful five-phase daily execution methodology that will create the cultural sustainability of Continuous Improvement. This is a methodology you will use as CEO at every level of your Continuous Improvement journey.
Bill Wallace
Success North Dallas, Founder & CEO

"John played the lead role in the design of our lean transformation. His design of super kaizen's that brought dramatic results in eight weeks or less contributed to the $175 million reductions that Dr. Pepper Snapple Group promise Wall Street. His ability to engage the organization is what makes him uniquely different from other lean practitioners."
Marty Ellen
Former CFO of Dr. Pepper Snapple Group

Rapid ROI

Mobilizing a Sustainable Improvement Journey

John Ballis
Lean Samurai

Foreword by
Norman Bodek

THiNKaha®

An Actionable Business Journal

E-mail: info@thinkaha.com
20660 Stevens Creek Blvd., Suite 210
Cupertino, CA 95014

Please go to
https://aha.pub/RapidROI
to read this AHAbook and to share the
individual AHA messages that resonate with you.

Published by THiNKaha®
20660 Stevens Creek Blvd., Suite 210,
Cupertino, CA 95014
https://thinkaha.com
E-mail: info@thinkaha.com

First Printing: January 2021
Hardcover ISBN: 978-1-61699-384-9   1-61699-384-7
Paperback ISBN: 978-1-61699-383-2   1-61699-383-9
eBook ISBN: 978-1-61699-382-5   1-61699-382-0
Place of Publication: Silicon Valley, California, USA
Paperback Library of Congress Number: 2020922692

Trademarks

All terms mentioned in this book that are known to be trademarks or service marks have been appropriately capitalized. Neither THiNKaha, nor any of its imprints, can attest to the accuracy of this information. Use of a term in this book should not be regarded as affecting the validity of any trademark or service mark.

Warning and Disclaimer

Every effort has been made to make this book as complete and as accurate as possible. The information provided is on an "as is" basis. The author(s), publisher, and their agents assume no responsibility for errors or omissions. Nor do they assume liability or responsibility to any person or entity with respect to any loss or damages arising from the use of information contained herein.

Dedication

This book is dedicated to anyone who has a learning disability, whether you are in a leadership role or not. Never let anyone hold you back, especially not yourself. You are special, and God has gifted you with unique talents. General Patton, one of my biggest heroes, was dyslexic. His mother never stopped believing in him. He flunked out of West Point his first year. But he never gave up, and through determination, grit, and belief, he became one of the greatest military leaders of all time.

"Never stop seeking out your dreams. Never let anyone stand in your way. Especially not yourself."

Acknowledgements

To say this book is by John Ballis would be an overstatement. The methodology that you will read about comes from the many mentors and influencers that I have had in my life. I have been fortunate to overcome several major disabilities. I am dyslexic and phonically deaf. Growing up, getting me from one grade to the next was always a major event. From the start of my career at IBM, I have been blessed by many great people who instilled the desire in my heart and soul to help companies continually improve.

At the top of my list is my family. I have truly been blessed to have an extraordinary group of extended family. These world leaders encouraged and inspired me throughout my career. The most significant person I would recognize is Ted Lakosky, one of my senior managers at IBM, who gave me my first big break. He told me that we need to utilize that gift of seeing things in reverse, or backward, to design our manufacturing lines. Being part of the nine-month effort that took making the PS2 gaming motherboard down from forty-five days' cycle time to four-and-a-half hours was a great honor and laid the foundation for my career. My second big break was when Michael George, founder of The George Group, brought me in to establish their implementation engineering staff. After five-and-a-half years, I was recruited by a window company to help turn it around utilizing my Lean skills. The George Group went on to become a world-class consulting firm implementing Lean and ultimately, Lean Six Sigma. At my new company, Jim Sardo took me underneath his wing and taught me the business and leadership skills that I needed to become a successful executive. I'm proud to say that after dedicating two-and-a-half years, this window company went from $183 million in sales to $360 million, in large part due to the culture of operational excellence that we built and the systems that we put in place.

These experiences formed the foundation for the methodology called M.A.R.I.S.—Mobilization, Assessment, Redesign, Implementation, and Sustainability—as an execution methodology for continuous improvement. Using M.A.R.I.S., I've had the privilege to travel the world and help over 100 companies implement a Lean journey in the world of continuous improvement.

I would be remiss if I did not mention other inspiring thought leaders who profoundly impacted my personal and professional development. Without them, I would not have created this valuable methodology.

Dr. Deming	Dr. Shingo	Philip Crosby
John Akers	Dr. Raymond T. Yeh	Dr. Tony Alexandra
Lou Holtz	Jack Welch	Don Washkewicz
Colin Powell	Norman Bodek	Fred Smith
Mike George	John Fox	K. John Fukuda

I thank all the employees over the years who have encouraged me, worked with me, and supported the development of this methodology that has saved billions of dollars for companies we've coached around the world.

I'd like to give special thanks to David Hamilton, one of the original proponents of integrating Lean and Six Sigma, for co-writing the preface and helping edit much of this book and for his contributions. His perspectives on continuous improvement in all its incarnations and his support over the years are greatly appreciated.

Lastly, a special thanks to First Lady Barbara Bush, who had a conference for dyslexic professionals that encouraged me to write my first book. Barbara told me, "Never be ashamed of the gift that God has given you." "Use it to help others" was her message that day. Those wise words have guided and strengthened me over the years.

How to Read a THiNKaha® Book

A Note from the Publisher

The AHAthat/THiNKaha series was crafted to deliver content the way humans process information in today's world. Short, sweet, and to the point while delivering powerful, lasting impact.

The content is designed and presented in ways to appeal to visual, auditory, and kinesthetic personality types. Each section contains AHA messages, lines for notes, and a meme that summarizes that section. You should also scan the QR code, or click on the link, to watch a video of the author talking about that section.

This book is contextual in nature. Although the words won't change, their meaning will every time you read it as your context will. Be ready, you will experience your own AHA moments as you read. The AHA messages are designed to be stand-alone actionable messages that will help you think differently. Items to consider as you're reading include:

1. It should only take less than an hour to read the first time. When you're reading, write one to three action items that resonate with you in the underlined areas.
2. Mark your calendar to re-read it again.
3. Repeat step #1 and mark one to three additional AHA messages that resonate. As they will most likely be different, this is a great time to reflect on the messages that resonated with you during your last reading.
4. Sprinkle credust on the author and yourself by sharing the AHA messages from this book socially from the AHAthat platform https://aha.pub/RapidROI.

After reading this THiNKaha book, marking your AHA messages, rereading it, and marking more AHA messages, you'll begin to see how this book contextually applies to you. We advocate for continuous, lifelong learning and this book will help you transform your AHAs into action items with tangible results.

Mitchell Levy, Global Credibility Expert

publisher@thinkaha.com

THiNKaha®

A THiNKaha book is not your typical book. It's a whole lot more, while being a whole lot less. Scan the QR code or use this link to watch me talk about this new evolutionary style of book: https://aha.pub/THiNKahaSeries

Contents

Foreword

As you read John's new book, have fun with it and take your pen and jot down all the wonderful ideas presented. Put people into study groups, and ask each person to read one chapter and to lead each study group session; ask each one a fundamental question: "How can we apply these execution methodologies and his ideas here?"

Many years ago, I owned Productivity Inc. and published many of the great leaders in this field. I had the honor to write for and publish many of the thought leaders' books in the world of continuous improvement and bring to the world many thought leaders from Japan, America, and the world. John Ballis is one of them. His book should move CEOs and leadership to execute change by following his proven execution methodologies to engage their people daily to eliminate waste in all processes.

John explains in simple terms how to create a journey to improve the organization's people, performance, and process improvement daily, as Ohno and Shingo did for Toyota. John wants you to write a simple but powerful vision to move your organization forward. Then, you need to change your people's performance plans so they align with the vision of the company. When CEOs and their organizations fully comply with his M.A.R.I.S. methodology, it will deliver an ROI daily on your continuous improvement journey.

I want you, as you read this book, to be like John and take the power of M.A.R.I.S., take out the key ideas that you get from this book, set new goals, and move your organizations forward to great success.

Look into your future, and envision what you want to personally be and how you want your company will look in the very near future to be successful and leave a legacy.

You start with your dream, you set great growth goals, you believe in your team and yourself that you have the skills and capabilities to attain those goals, and you gain support from others. You challenge your associates to get excited doing what they want to do to reach that great common success.

John's ideas should inspire you to fulfill that dream.

I wish you the best of luck on your continuous improvement journey.

Norman Bodek
Godfather of Lean

Preface — The History and Future of the Lean Journey

Ultimately, it was leadership and culture that enabled military, technological, and economic breakthroughs. It was also leadership and culture that enabled certain countries to sustain the drive for innovation, efficiency, productivity, and excellence. Fundamentally, David Hamilton and I and many others argue that it was leadership and culture that enabled the military, technological, and economic breakthroughs that built those nations. It was also leadership and culture that enabled those countries to sustain their success.

Leadership produced cultures driven to innovate and become more efficient, productive, and successful. Ultimately, it was failures of leadership and the weakening and eventual destruction of their cultures that lead to the downfall of their civilizations.

The Industrial Revolution's use of interchangeable parts and specialization of labor is a familiar example. It is credited for the sun not setting on the British Empire for over 100 years. People may not realize that a standard design for crossbows and interchangeable parts centuries before helped Emperor Chin create an unstoppable fighting force out of untrained peasants and rise to power, leading to the creation of China. The Mongol's use of lightning-fast, coordinated cavalry enabled Genghis Khan to conquer the largest expanse ever seen. The Spartan Phalanx, with their long spears and heavy shields, made them the most fearsome fighting force of their time. The Roman military and their systems of management, logistics, and sanitation, along with the arch and cement, helped build an empire.

What fundamental thing produced these societies? Did they enjoy special resources or a strategic geographic advantage? A case can be made that in some cases, those things can influence success. None of the examples above had an abundance of natural resources. Moreover, many leading economists, sociologists, and anthropologists argue that great natural resources have an inverse relationship to advancement and competitive advantage.

The Japanese proved this.

Japan after World War II was decimated: it had no money, few natural resources, little land, and a horrific economic depression. Some would argue that it was the lack of these resources that forced the Japanese to become incredibly efficient. A lack of land and money made holding inventory costly. They could produce a hundred cars, ship them, and wait to get paid. They needed to build them as efficiently as possible.

Some would also say that it was Japan's culture, which valued hard work, sacrifice, determination, efficiency, cooperation, and pride in workmanship, that made Japan's rise from the ashes possible. Certainly, the Marshall Plan and the War Acts certainly helped. But there have been countless examples of other countries that received enormous aid and never achieved great success. Many of them have become dependent on it and remain in poverty. Ultimately, it was the Japanese culture and its people's willingness to do anything and use anything necessary to build itself back up that created its success.

I think that we all agree that "stick-to-it-iveness," if that is a word, is absolutely critical to success in any endeavor. Multiple studies have shown convincingly that grit is more important than any other factor in personal success—so, as it stands to reason, it should be so for organizational success. Grit, which is a vital attribute of great leadership in combination with self-awareness, honesty, accountability, genuine caring, and humility, is required to make a great leader and great corporate leadership. Gritty cultures win.

Culture is defined by some as, "what you care about and what you care for." While music, food, fashion, dance, decorations, language, customs, etc. are clearly part of one's culture, at its foundation, culture is your nation's DNA. That DNA is made up of values, belief systems, habits, behavioral norms, communication styles, leadership approaches, etc. Let's be clear: it was culture that enabled all the examples above to achieve success—values, not natural resources, and leadership, not luck, and people with the purpose to follow the standard process and procedures. Culture created the success and sustained it or let it die.

If we care about or value something, we will pay for it, right? Related to this, people have said, "Be careful what you pay for . . . you'll get it." The story of Ross Perot Sr. serves as a great cautionary tale. As IBM's top salesman, Ross made more than the president. The company reacted by capping his compensation. By the end of the first quarter, his income was capped. With too much free time on his hands, too much talent, and too much ambition, he left to create EDS. IBM's culture couldn't accept a salesperson making more than its leader. It cared for and paid for positional authority and prestige, not results. And that's what they got.

Countless other innovators and successful leaders have had to find the right environment to flourish, the right culture. If they couldn't find it, they had to create it. It is hard to imagine Henry Ford, Steve Jobs, Bill Gates, or Michael Dell achieving their success in another time period or country. They had to find or create the right environment to flourish. Having said that, though, wouldn't we prefer that these kinds of contributors and leaders stay with our firms? How do we create a culture supportive of "entrepreneurs"?

In business, numerous approaches and tools have been developed for companies to make better decisions, eliminate waste, speed up innovation, engage employees, etc. This pursuit of an integrated, holistic, all-encompassing system that solves every problem is what I refer to as "The Way."

Deming's SPC helped the Japanese become a dominant force in manufacturing and electronics. That evolved into Quality Circles, JIT, the Toyota Production System, Lean, Six Sigma, Lean Six Sigma, Agile, and many other business methodologies, tool sets, and philosophies. We believe strongly that Lean and all its related approaches are really one philosophy, parts of a greater whole. Our experience has taught us that in the operational excellence/LSS world, the focus has been, to our mind, too much on tools and too little on mindset, purpose, norms, philosophy, etc. Ultimately, "The Way" to succeed is based on culture/ leadership, not tools or techniques.

"Lean Your Way" is based on the idea that no two companies, no two cultures, are the same.

The formula for success has been different throughout time. But the fundamental and pervasive factor that has enabled great competitive advantage is culture. Our ultimate assertion is that the organization (be it a country or a business) that gets the most out of its people wins—period. These are the ones that provide the right environment: incentives, opportunities, tools, motivation, autonomy, standards, principles, and values. Whatever approaches you take on your Lean journey must fit your people's way of thinking and their values. It must be "Lean Your Way."

Each organization's approach to implementing Lean should be different. No two companies, industries, or business environments are the same. They must develop Lean based on their company's DNA. They must also accept that despite business thinking being fickle and management consulting being a "fashion industry," no new shiny toy will ensure success. An integrated approach to using tools that increase efficiency and quality, underpinned by a philosophy and culture of continuous improvement and empowerment of people, is the only way to secure a competitive advantage in the long run. Call it whatever you want—Agile, if it makes you happy.

Lean isn't complicated. It's just hard. Like anything worthwhile, it takes work. A journey of a thousand miles begins with a single step, and it ends when you stop moving your feet. Beginning or renewing your journey can create a legacy for generations to come. The benefits, or ROI, of your journey can be huge. They can come rapidly. And they can be sustained. All it needs is leadership with a vision and commitment and the ability to communicate that vision.

#ContinuousImprovement affects the EBITDA in such a positive way that the corporation will:
1) stand out from the competition and
2) continually meet or exceed its goals.

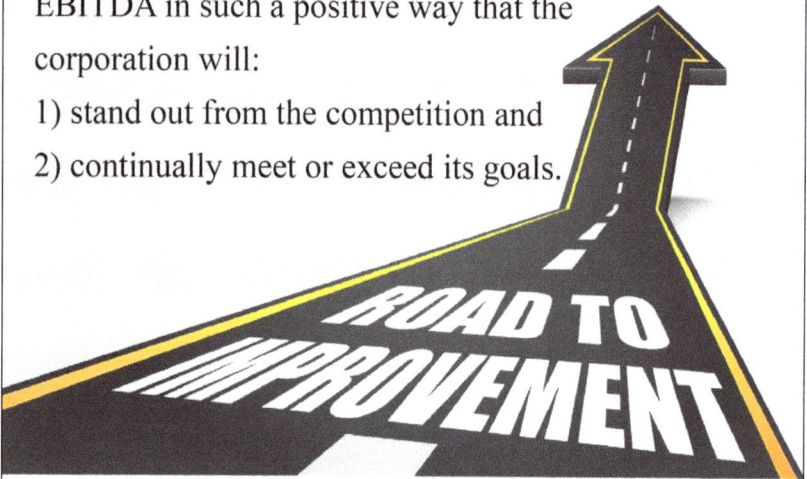

ROAD TO IMPROVEMENT

John Ballis
https://aha.pub/RapidROI

Share the AHA messages from this book socially by going to
https://aha.pub/RapidROI.

Scan the QR code or use this link to watch the section videos and more on this section topic:
https://aha.pub/RapidROISVs

Section I

Introduction — Creation of a Sustainable Journey for Continuous Improvement

Every corporation wanting to survive and thrive must learn to sustain continuous improvement (CI) and remain committed to its journey in partnership with engaged employees.

Does a successfully sustained commitment to Lean guarantee success and survival 100% of the time? No.

Having said that, we can't point to any company with bad service, bad design, bad quality, high costs, etc. that survives, let alone thrives. Lean is foundational, a must-have.

In a business world that keeps evolving, competitors aggressively find ways to replace what's great with something greater. We all acknowledge that corporations that choose to stay the same are bound to lose. Hitting your targets today is not a guarantee of sustaining competitiveness. Good is never good enough. The key to remaining competitive is a vision, commitment, and a dedicated methodology for continuous improvement that happens every day at every level throughout all areas of a business.

A simple way to look at this is how all those firms renowned for operational excellence thrive and survive for a very long time. Sometimes, radical change happens and tech becomes obsolete. We've seen disruptive tech do this thousands of times. However, we have seen many companies with resilient leadership and cultures that adapt. They see change happening and they innovate. Change is inevitable. Either adapt and overcome or perish. This is true Lean Culture.

What do you believe?

My survey of CEOs and leadership on the success and failure of Lean implementations is a foundational element of this book and M.A.R.I.S. Look at the diagram below to see if you can find your company in the journey.

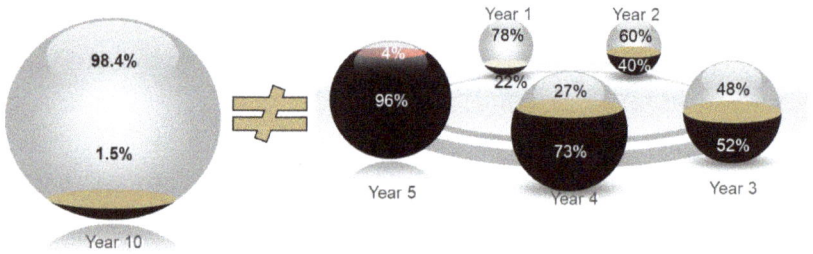

Sustainment Reasons for Failure of Lean/Six Sigma & Continuous Improvement from 1000 Fortune 500 Companies Leaders (12,000 total responses) in a 2012 Survey by John Ballis

Only 4 percent of all companies make the transformation sustainable within five years, and only 1.5 percent of companies make the achievement sustainable past ten years. Even companies that received recognitions, such as the Shingo Prize, Best Manufacturing, ASQ, AME, Industrial Engineers, LSS World, and others, in many cases, they did not sustain the organizational structure and best improvement practices that earned them the awards. Only 2 percent have sustained the journey of continuous improvement. That is leadership and culture.

To believe it's possible, it's important to look at successful companies. Toyota has been leading the way with a great operational system that works for them—their way. Their accomplishment is even more remarkable given that only 1.5 percent of documented leaders in Lean movement maintain their success for over ten years. Toyota has done this for over sixty years.

Are there things that Toyota could do better? Yes. Recently, they have said that they won't build boring cars any longer. Their management team, their leadership, understands that CI must happen everywhere, not just for transactional situations and shop floor manufacturing and not just in quality. CI can apply to strategy, innovation, R&D, marketing, branding, sales, and M&A—everywhere.

What kind of Lean leader are you?

One fundamental question that all leaders considering a Lean journey must ask themselves is this: "If we apply ourselves, will we achieve our goal?" Do you believe in it?

All too often, business leaders have looked for a silver bullet, a panacea, that will fix all their problems. When their implementation of an approach doesn't work, they tend to blame the approach and not their implementation. Many of us are good at this. "The diet was to blame or the exercise regime, or both were to blame, not me!"

In my opinion, there are only two kinds of leaders with respect to sustaining Lean and all its variants. David Hamilton's "Lean Leader Tree" is a valuable way to look at this. Lean leaders are:

1. Those who have tried CI
2. Those who haven't tried CI
   o Of those who have tried CI, there are two types:
     • Those who have succeeded
     • Those who have failed or have not gotten the result or the ROI they expected
       • Of those who have failed, there are two types:
         • Those who are poorly led by consultants and let the consultants led the implementation for CI, and then blame them
         • Those who do a bad job and take responsibility for it not working when they picked the wrong people internally

If you don't believe that Lean works, if you don't believe that it takes work, and if you don't believe that the effort is worth it, don't start. In all things, ROI matters. We do those things that we believe will give us the highest ROI because we choose to be on a journey of continuous improvement.

What your people believe is what matters

It was surprising to many participating CEOs that poor communication, not tools, etc., was the number-one reason for failure. Good communication reflects and secures commitment. Where little or no communication takes place, there will not be commitment and there will be failure.

Belief and commitment start with the CEO or top leadership: your employees are a simple reflection of your leadership. They believe what you believe and what you communicate. Anyone can make a mistake. Jack Welch once said that if he had done it all over again, he would not have had a program of Lean/Six Sigma with green, black, and master belts. He would have created an internal title and a GE name for the journey. Every time that GE had a package to downsize, they lost their best people with Lean/Six Sigma certifications because the industry's new GE had a good program. This is why when I was at Dr. Pepper Snapple Group, we created an internal title and called the journey, Rapid Continuous Improvement. The leadership must mobilize around the creation of the journey first so they can live it and people will follow.

CEOs must learn how to mobilize their employees to assess where they are right now, redesign their process and culture to keep up with the competition, implement the redesigned process, and sustain it as the new standard of work. This cycle must happen repeatedly, from the root level to the top, so continuous improvement can become part of the corporation's DNA.

CEOs must be willing to improve themselves continually, and employees must be highly engaged to play their part. Motivating and engaging employees are the only ways to remain relevant, competitive, and industry leading.

1

Every corporation has to continually improve because the competition is not sitting idle. Any corporation that doesn't care about #ContinuousImprovement will soon be obsolete.

_____

_____

_____

2

The competition is doing some form of #ContinuousImprovement every day.
Corporations that are not creating something more sustainable than their competitors are bound to lose.

_____

_____

_____

3

The change of culture and processes toward #ContinuousImprovement has to happen at every level. But it has to start at the top: from the CEO.

_____

_____

_____

4

The CEO, the managers, and the employees are the best engineers who can implement #ContinuousImprovement in their corporation. They can come together to redesign their process and make it better.

_____

_____

_____

5

A corporation that does not #ContinuallyImprove will never become the superstar they're meant to be. Their cost will continually deplete their cash flow. Their employees will never be engaged to reduce cost and improve work on a daily basis.

_____

_____

_____

6

With #ContinuousImprovement, employees will be
empowered to eliminate the non-value-adds
because they take pride in what they do.

_____

_____

_____

7

When #ContinuousImprovement is in the corporation's
DNA, employees deliver the best quality because they
know where the non-value-adds are.

_____

_____

_____

8

For some corporations, quality is number one. But even with the best quality, if they don't deliver product on time, complete, and at the right cost, they will not be able to stay in the supply chain. #ContinuousImprovement

_____

_____

_____

9

Corporations that #ContinuallyImprove:
1) reduce costs, 2) improve quality, and
3) maintain on-time and complete delivery
to customers.

_____

_____

_____

10

#ContinuousImprovement affects the EBITDA in such a
positive way that the corporation will: 1) stand out from
the competition and 2) continually meet or exceed
its goals.

_____

_____

_____

To discover the #ROI opportunities, the CEO needs to understand how the corporation is doing today. A visual value stream map can help because it reveals the value-adds and the non-value-adds in the current process.

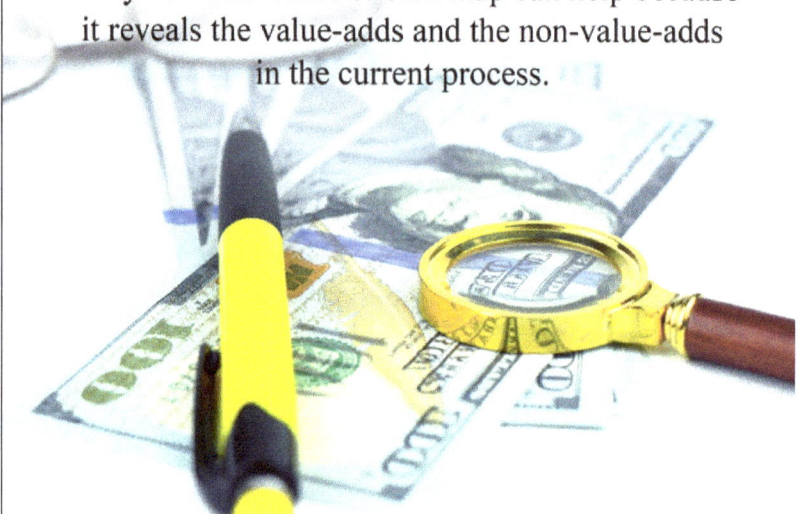

John Ballis
https://aha.pub/RapidROI

Share the AHA messages from this book socially by going to
https://aha.pub/RapidROI.

Scan the QR code or use this link to watch the section videos and more on this section topic:
https://aha.pub/RapidROISVs

Section II

Discovery of the ROI Opportunities

When managers and employees are too focused on their daily operations, they tend to forget the importance of continuous improvement. Their job isn't simply to run a business. They must see their role as supporting employees to improve the business daily. Those employees will find ways to improve the business and generate ROI. Leadership's job is to empower employees to find those ways, give them the resources that they need to implement them, and reward and recognize them so they continue to do it. We all must work in business (daily operations) and on the business (continuous improvement). World-class organizations do both. It can be hard at times, but you can make it fun if you choose.

CEOs must focus their time on removing the top four reasons for failure.

Number 1. Organizational Communication

- What's the vision of the journey? How are you going to communicate? The communications must come from the CEO, as the leader of the journey to greatness. Great CEOs lead from the front, not the middle or the back, nor do they delegate it to a staff member. They are involved, from communicating the vision to living Lean every day and letting everyone know that they have a role in the journey. The companies that are in the 2 percent after ten years have leadership on the frontlines, participating in continuous improvement themselves. They are great servant leaders.

Number 2. False Starts

- The organization is not ready for the change because the vision has not been communicated correctly. Employees are confused because their performance plans reward them for the behavior of making the numbers. The plans must change to avoid this failure. Employees are thinking, "Here we go again, another program of the month."

Number 3. Engagement Alignment

- You need to allow people to make changes within their own process. Too many managers and CI leaders are control freaks. Leadership selects the wrong person to lead a journey 57 percent of the time. The behavioral personality type is key. This person does not have to be the expert in the tools of Lean, but they need to be the super coach to keep the journey moving forward at all levels.

Number 4. Resistance of Employees

- People fear the unknown, so avoid that by communicating the vision and changing your performance plans to align their behaviors. The greatest fear is, "Will I lose my job?" Let attrition be your friend, and let performance plans remove the people from the organization who are holding it back from greatness.

Great CEOs realize that the ultimate ROI of continuous improvement is an engaged culture that flows throughout the corporation and has an improved process designed by their own team. When the supervisors, managers, and employees are all working toward achieving greatness, ROI becomes sustainable.

This section reveals the ROI of continuous improvement. With this, any corporation can stand above the rest in the midst of continually evolving competition.

11

Corporations that are too focused on day-to-day activities are missing out on the consistent #ROI of #ContinuousImprovement. They may even lose profit.

_____

_____

_____

12

The #ROI of #ContinuousImprovement comes from saving money through a highly engaged culture. This culture mobilizes employees to reduce cost and improve quality every single day.

_____

_____

_____

13

Discovering the #ROI opportunities is understanding how to convert Lean concepts, #ContinuousImprovement, and sustainability into cash.

_____

_____

_____

14

CEOs want a continuous #ROI without having to reinvest on new processes. Investing in new processes takes away from the corporation's profitability. #ContinuousImprovement

_____

_____

_____

15

Most CEOs repeat the same sin all the time: If what they have doesn't work, they'll look for a replacement when they should be going for an #ROI.

_____

_____

_____

16

CEOs can only say that there's an #ROI if they use the same methodology and it consistently earns them a return on investment every year.

_____

_____

_____

17

CEOs don't need to spend millions of dollars to bring consultants in for an #ROI discovery. CEOs, managers, and employees can discover #ROI opportunities on their own.

_____

_____

_____

18

Discovering #ROI opportunities requires every CEO to 1) clarify what their vision is and 2) find out if it is being achieved in the corporation.

_____

_____

_____

19

A visual value stream map enables the CEO to see what's happening at the supervisory level, at the management level, and at the operational level. #ContinuousImprovement

_____

_____

_____

20

To discover the #ROI opportunities, the CEO needs to understand how the corporation is doing today. A visual value stream map can help because it reveals the value-adds and the non-value-adds in the current process.

_____

_____

_____

21

A visual value stream map reveals employee behaviors
that cause defects. By uncovering these flaws,
CEOs will see what needs to be improved.

_____

_____

_____

22

In #ROI discovery, CEOs and managers need to assess
employee performance and find out: 1) if employees are
doing well and 2) which areas of work employees need
help with.

_____

_____

_____

23

Once the CEO and the manager understand how employees are doing, 1) they can empower them to #ContinuallyImprove and 2) they can provide help where help is needed. #ROI

_____

_____

_____

24

When employees feel valued, they are encouraged to perform better. This boosts employee engagement, which is an #ROI of #ContinuousImprovement.

_____

_____

_____

25

#ContinuousImprovement can take the corporation to the next level by enabling its business process and employee culture to earn a consistent #ROI annually.

_____

_____

_____

Through #Mobilization, managers are trained to stop being a leader-supervisor and start being a coach-mentor. Being a coach-mentor means leading by example.

John Ballis
https://aha.pub/RapidROI

Share the AHA messages from this book socially by going to
https://aha.pub/RapidROI.

Scan the QR code or use this link to watch the section videos and more on this section topic:
https://aha.pub/RapidROISVs

Section III

Mobilization

When employees don't feel valued, they can't be mobilized to help the corporation. Mobilization is vital because the corporation only has their employees to rely on for continuous improvement.

Managers must know how to capture the input, creativity, and know-how of their employees. They must create mechanisms and standard practices to do this.

How do we communicate our vision? How do we get their input? How do we convince them that we are serious? How do we communicate that we will value them and take action? How do we give them what they need to improve their work processes? How do we keep them from fearing that they will lose their job if they make things more efficient? What's in it for them? Answering these questions is how we generate the energy and commitment needed for employees to contribute and perform their best to achieve the new vision for the journey.

Mobilization is made perfect when everyone in the whole corporation uses their energy to eliminate waste in their processes. When they know where the non-value-added activities are, they can focus their energy on eliminating them to improve production in every function of the business. Every day, your team will create a mobilization around people, performance, and process improvement. They will start with people and review safety. Then, they will do a performance review of deliveries made on time, complete quality as defined by customers, and the cost to create a profit. Process improvement will focus on can do's" and "need help's to remove waste. This is done daily around a visual management board, whether a physical white board or an electronic one. It's called a daily huddle and reviews, "Did we win yesterday or did we lose? How can we change the play to create a winning day?" This is why mobilization sets you up for greatness.

Mobilized employees who can create a sustained state of continuous improvement for the corporation is the super goal for it to become great.

26

Corporations only have their employees to rely on for #ContinuousImprovement. If employees don't feel valued, CEOs and managers cannot #Mobilize them to perform better.

_____

_____

_____

27

The most important phase of #ContinuousImprovement is #Mobilization. It requires CEOs to: 1) create a reflection of what great looks like, 2) communicate it well to employees, and 3) energize them every day to achieve it.

_____

_____

_____

28

#Mobilization does not create a sense of fear. It creates a sense of energy and enjoyment of being part of the team.

_____

_____

_____

29

Without #Mobilization, the employees will not have self-awareness of their behaviors, and the corporation will not be able to make any lasting improvement.

_____

_____

_____

30

#Mobilization is about calling people to action. When employees can't be mobilized, they can't be energized to make any lasting improvement.

_____

_____

_____

31

#Mobilization is about energizing everybody to 1) be at their best, 2) outperform what's expected of them, and 3) enjoy it along the way.

_____

_____

_____

32

#Mobilization is all about creating that energy in the team as if they're going into the game that could get them to the playoffs.

33

#Mobilization is being able to call employees 1) to produce better quality and 2) to prevent accidents from happening.

34

Part of #Mobilization is making sure that employees are safe while they work. Managers have to make sure that hazards don't exist in the corporation.

_____

_____

_____

35

#Mobilization involves making managers conscious of their negative talk. Positive talk best mobilizes employees to action.

_____

_____

_____

36

If you tear people down, then don't expect anything in return except to be torn down as a leader. —Lou Holtz via https://aha.pub/JohnBallis #Mobilization

---

37

The critical factor for #Mobilization is the ability of managers to convert negative behaviors into positive ones that reinforce what they want.

38

Managers should approach faults with open-ended questions like, "What went wrong?" instead of, "Who was wrong?" This way, they can call employees to action by leading them to become self-aware.

_____

_____

_____

39

When managers call out "what" went wrong instead of "who" was wrong, employees are mobilized to change for the better. #Mobilization

_____

_____

_____

40

#Mobilization creates a Hawthorne effect for the positive. When managers are positive and encouraging, 1) employees are mobilized and 2) productivity goes up.

_____

_____

_____

41

Managers must see to it that the corporation is a good environment for the employees. They should be able to get to work, and there shouldn't be high absenteeism. #Mobilization

_____

_____

_____

42

Through #Mobilization, managers are trained to stop
being a leader-supervisor and start being a coach-
mentor. Being a coach-mentor means leading
by example.

_____

_____

_____

43

Managers can #Mobilize employees if they teach through demonstration. When something needs to be taken care of, the manager must be ready to take care of it.

44

Energized employees create a highly engaged culture that CEOs need from their workforce. This culture sustains a state of #ContinuousImprovement for the corporation. #Mobilization

---

If the #Assessment is done right, the value stream map will morph over time. Value-added activities will increase, while non-value-added activities will decrease.

John Ballis
https://aha.pub/RapidROI

Share the AHA messages from this book socially by going to
https://aha.pub/RapidROI.

Scan the QR code or use this link to watch the section videos and more on this section topic:
https://aha.pub/RapidROISVs

Section IV

Assessment

Mobilization is just one part of continuous improvement in the M.A.R.I.S. system. Even when the CEO can energize and unite their employees, they still need a direction for how they will arrive at a great destination.

Assessment is that essential part of continuous improvement where the CEO, managers, and employees sit down together to assess where they are right now—honestly.

By assessing where the processes in the corporation are today, they can create a roadmap of how to reduce the non-value-adds and increase efficiency that creates value for the customers and shareholders in the future.

In a continuous improvement journey, this roadmap is a common communication tool called a value stream map. It breaks down the process and classifies activities into value-adds and non-value-adds in such a way that everyone at every level understands them at a glance. Learning to see is not just building a map in a conference room; it's going to the owner's functions and processes and even going to the floor to see it. The owner of the value stream must be involved in collecting the data and signing off on what is true, even if it does not match the standard.

Once the employees learn to see and understand where the non-value-adds are, they will know where to focus their energy. This is done daily to meet customer requirements and make improvements. In a value stream map, the blue is value-added, and the pink is non-value-added processes. I want leaders to see an ocean of pink. I want the organizations to understand that there is too much non-value in every process. In fact, it's Little's Law that tells us that most workflows are less than 2 percent efficient. Shingo said that until you get to 50 percent value add and 50 percent non-value add, then you're on a journey to eliminate waste. We assess every day how we did the day before. When we have failures, we should be able to find it on our value stream map. If it is at the top of the Pareto graph, then the team will focus on it in Redesign.

45

#Assessment is required so the managers and employees will have a roadmap to a great destination. Without proper assessment, their drive to improve will be wasted.

_____

_____

_____

46

#Assessment is bringing the process to life. It requires an effective way of communicating to everybody at every level so they will be aligned about what's important and what's not.

_____

_____

_____

47

In #Assessment, a value stream map is created to show the workflow required to come up with a product or service. It classifies activities as value-add or non-value-add.

_____

_____

_____

48

A value stream map is full of processes and tasks that either bring value to the end goal or don't. #Assessment

_____

_____

_____

49

A value stream map is a communication tool that identifies wastes. Wastes are the non-value-adds, while productive activities are the value-adds.

_____

_____

_____

50

A value stream map is what managers and employees use to work together so waste can be removed. #Assessment

_____

_____

_____

51

The most dangerous kind of waste is the waste
we do not recognize. —Shigeo Shingo
via https://aha.pub/JohnBallis #Assessment

_____

_____

_____

52

Unfortunately, a value stream map is usually 98%
non-value-add versus only 2% value-add. There is
much more waste than productive parts of a process.
#Assessment

_____

_____

_____

53

Shingo said that if corporations want to be world class, their value stream map should be 50% value-added activities and 50% non-value-added activities. #Assessment

_____

_____

_____

54

#Assessment is powerful because it brings value streams to life. It creates a color communication code of value-added and non-value-added activities that the team can understand and work on.

_____

_____

_____

55

If employees in the corporation see value-adds versus non-value-adds the same way, managers can get them to focus on the "right" things to do. #Assessment

_____

_____

_____

56

When value-adds and non-value-adds are identified, the employees can drill down to the root cause and eliminate the waste. #Assessment

_____

_____

_____

57

Value stream maps are done in colors: yellow for processes, baby blue for value-adds, and pink for non-value-adds. When the team sees a huge cluster of pink, they can be mobilized to work on it. #Assessment

_____

_____

_____

58

Managers who are able to 1) spot the non-value-adds and 2) mobilize employees to remove them are on their way to a #ContinuousImprovement journey. #Assessment

_____

_____

_____

59

#Assessment brings a common language for clear communication. It guarantees ROI by enabling the employees to eliminate the non-value-adds.

_____

_____

_____

60

If the #Assessment is done right, the value stream map will morph over time. Value-added activities will increase, while non-value-added activities will decrease.

_____

_____

_____

61

Everybody in the corporation will see where the non-value-adds are if the #Assessment was done properly. This enables them to focus their energy on eliminating the waste.

_____

_____

_____

When a corporation #Redesigns its process, it will either reduce product costs or labor costs. Either way, it'll improve productivity that leads to a tangible ROI.

Organizational Culture and Attitudes

Processes

Coordination and Collaboration

Value Chain Management

Leadership

Employees

Technology Investment

John Ballis
https://aha.pub/RapidROI

Share the AHA messages from this book socially by going to
https://aha.pub/RapidROI.

Scan the QR code or use this link to watch the section videos and more on this section topic:
https://aha.pub/RapidROISVs

Section V

Redesign

Finding the non-value-add in processes is not enough to ensure continuous improvement. CEOs, managers, and employees still need to come up with a better process, where waste is eliminated.

This section talks about the critical steps to redesign. It's where the corporation discovers the best changes to be implemented so the non-value-add can truly be removed. This not just for the processes. It is for redesigning how Leadership interfaces with employees and how performance plans should reflect servant leadership at every level. How do you redesign the technology to mirror the new workflows? AI technologies should be used to validate value stream maps and uncover gold nuggets for redesign.

Redesign isn't about using fancy tools. It's about using the right tools at the right time by the right people trained to use them and nothing more. Simple is better. Fast is better.

Redesign is all about extracting the best ideas from the team, capturing them, communicating them, and evaluating the best ones to be implemented for improvement. Redesign is not about spending capital to improve the process. Shigeo Shingo created SMED (single minute dye exchange or change over reduction) without spending any capital at Toyota. It's fine for companies to spend capital, but it should come from ROI by eliminating the current waste to offset or pay for the new capital.

Creating tangible ROI through redesign is exciting and motivating to managers and employees, giving them a new-found sense of pride and accomplishment. They will have ownership of the new process that they built, which creates a new culture in the corporation, one of high employee engagement that makes continuous improvement sustainable.

62

There can be no #ContinuousImprovement if non-value-adds are still present in daily operations. The business process needs to be #Redesigned so waste cannot exist.

_____

_____

_____

63

#Redesign is about 1) improving the process to delight customers, 2) changing employee behaviors for the better, and 3) creating a sustainable journey of #ContinuousImprovement.

_____

_____

_____

64

The DNA of every corporation may be unique. But each one needs a #Redesign to 1) improve cash flow and 2) engage employees for better performance.

_____

_____

_____

65

#Redesign involves: 1) eliminating waste in the process and 2) creating a new and improved design to attain the CEO's desired ROI.

66

#Redesign is looking at the ideas that will be the most impactful to the business and setting them up for #Implementation.

67

The tangible ROI of #Redesign is cost reduction, while the non-tangible ROI is a higher level of employee engagement.

_____

_____

_____

68

In an ordinary corporation, employees are 10% naysayers, 10% highly engaged, and 80% in between. #Redesign can convert the 80% in-betweens and the 10% naysayers into the 10% highly engaged employees.

_____

_____

_____

69

Through #Redesign, naysayers can be engaged by empowering them to contribute and make positive changes for the corporation.

70

Benchmarking before #Redesigning is important. It reveals the wrong paradigm of the corporation to promote self-awareness.

71

#Redesign is essentially doing a paradigm shift so the corporation will have an improved cash flow and an engaged culture.

72

#Redesigning the process reveals whether the managers and employees did the #Assessment correctly. Were they able to identify the value-adds and non-value adds correctly — or not?

73

In #Redesign, the team needs to: 1) set a design goal,
2) identify if the current process is working, and
3) get down to the root cause of the issues.

_____

_____

_____

74

The team needs to find out where time is wasted in the process. This will result in a bigger yield, reduction of time, and increased productivity. #Redesign

_____

_____

_____

75

When a corporation #Redesigns its process, it will either reduce product costs or labor costs. Either way, it'll improve productivity that leads to a tangible ROI.

_____

_____

_____

76

By looking at the non-relevant parts of the process and thinking about how to eliminate them, the team will generate great ideas for implementation. #Redesign

_____

_____

_____

77

#Redesign brings out brilliant ideas that weren't thought of before. It creates pride of ownership among the employees.

_____

_____

_____

78

While doing a #Redesign, the team should always capture everyone's ideas, regardless if they get into the list for implementation.

_____

_____

_____

79

When ideas from employees are logged during the #Redesign phase, they will feel valued.

_____

_____

_____

80

When everybody's ideas get captured, it creates an environment where everybody wants to contribute. This results in another level of employee engagement. #Redesign

_____

_____

_____

81

Generating the most impactful ideas from the team will create a whole new layer of engagement. Employee engagement leads to a new layer of ROI for the corporation. #Redesign

_____

_____

_____

82

Employee behaviors need to be #Redesigned too. After redesigning the process, managers need to redesign the environment by encouraging employees to take action.

_____

_____

_____

83

The final step of #Redesign is doing a small pilot rollout to make sure that the team captured everything that could be done to improve the process.

_____

_____

_____

84

After the #Redesign, 1) tweaks can be made to improve the process, and 2) employees will have a sense of ownership and a desire to #ContinuouslyImprove.

_____

_____

_____

#Implementation has to be done as rapidly as possible to prevent the grass from growing back. If the team trimmed something out in redesign but didn't implement it rapidly, it cannot be sustained.

Time Management

Quality Management

Communications Management

Cost Management

Change Management

Project Execution

Procurement Management

Risk Management

Acceptance Management

Issue Management

John Ballis
https://aha.pub/RapidROI

Share the AHA messages from this book socially by going to
https://aha.pub/RapidROI.

Scan the QR code or use this link to watch the section videos and more on this section topic:
https://aha.pub/RapidROISVs

Section VI

Implementation

Without a rapid and proper implementation of the redesigned process, the "grass" will definitely grow back.

Employees will return to their old ways of doing things. Unproductive behaviors will return to poison the culture. The naysayers will gain momentum because failure in implementation will validate their cynical attitude toward an improved culture.

If CEOs want to attain the ROI of continuous improvement, they have to quickly set the redesigned process as the new standard of work and the positive employee behaviors as the new culture. This means employee performance plans have to drive this new behavior. A simple measure of implementation is the speed at which ideas are implemented. The cycle time reduction metric can be applied here. (Exit's / WIP (Ideas created in Redesign) = cycle time (speed to implementation)). This holds management accountable for getting it done versus just talking about it.

Implementation is crucial because if done right, it will allow the corporation to not only attain but also sustain the ROI of continuous improvement. This section discusses how to draw a clear implementation plan that will rapidly deploy the positive changes out of redesign.

Once the managers and the employees succeed in implementing the redesigned process, they are one step away from sustaining continuous improvement.

85

Proper #Implementation of the #Redesigned process is important to prevent the grass from growing back. What the corporation needs is a solid and rapid implementation plan.

_____

_____

_____

86

Every CEO needs a realistic #Implementation plan that is: 1) attainable and 2) effective in delivering real results.

_____

_____

_____

87

#Implementation is setting a new standard of work based on the redesigned process and culture. It can create a complete paradigm shift for the whole corporation.

_____

_____

_____

88

#Implementation should be done by the employees, not by some engineers or consultants.

_____

_____

_____

89

#Implementing a process that the employees created is better than bringing a consultant to create a process for them. If a CEO does the latter, employees will start pointing fingers as soon as the process goes wrong.

_____

_____

_____

90

What's good with #ContinuousImprovement is that the employees take ownership of the process they created. When something goes wrong in the #Implementation phase, they won't point fingers.

_____

_____

_____

91

Without the employees' pride of owning the process, the "grass" will definitely grow back. Unproductive behaviors and wastes in the process will return. #Implementation

_____

_____

_____

92

The #Implementation plan must be clear and detailed so everyone will understand it. This will make the redesigned process easier to carry out.

_____

_____

_____

93

The #Implementation plan must have a timeframe that allows rapid deployment of changes.

_____

_____

_____

94

Rapid #Implementation is critical. If this is not done, the naysayers will be the voice of the corporation saying that #ContinuousImprovement is never meant to work.

_____

_____

_____

95

#Implementation has to be done as rapidly as possible to prevent the grass from growing back. If the team trimmed something out in redesign but didn't implement it rapidly, it cannot be sustained.

_____

_____

_____

96

It's critical for the #Implementation phase to be rapid and measurable. Otherwise, the old habits and processes will come back.

_____

_____

_____

97

If the #Implementation phase is not rapid and measurable: 1) CEOs and managers will shoot aimlessly, and 2) employees will return to their old habits.

_____

_____

_____

98

In #Implementation, CEOs must understand that ownership needs to happen at the root level. Otherwise, the ROI will never come to fruition.

_____

_____

_____

99

In #Implementation, employees work together to improve the process. This creates pride of ownership, which then gives birth to sustainability.

100

The power of #Implementation is that the employees can get so excited about what they created and take pride in it.

101

When the team sits down and discusses how to improve their processes, they can come up with the most brilliant ideas. When these ideas are finally #Implemented, productivity goes up.

_____

_____

_____

102

If the employees have a sense of ownership and take pride in the new process, they will be happy to #Implement and sustain it.

_____

_____

_____

103

#Implementation delivers tangible ROI, positive financial impact, and non-tangible ROI, creating a highly engaged culture.

_____

_____

_____

104

With proper #Implementation, employees take pride in the redesigned process. It creates a culture of engagement and ownership that makes them willing to #ContinuallyImprove.

_____

_____

_____

If a culture of trust is created in the corporation, employees will feel comfortable to do what they know is right. This will empower them to deliver more than what's asked from them — more than what the CEOs think they need. #Sustainability

John Ballis
https://aha.pub/RapidROI

Share the AHA messages from this book socially by going to
https://aha.pub/RapidROI.

Scan the QR code or use this link to watch the section videos and more on this section topic:
https://aha.pub/RapidROISVs

Section VII

Sustainability

A corporation content merely to hit its goals in a machine-like fashion will eventually fail. Only by working with employees to continuously change and improve the entire business can a company hope to get ahead of the competition to ensure that they stay in business with a legacy. To do this, they must build trust with their employees. Their employees must not see their job as something to clock into every day. Instead, they should want to take ownership of their job and know that its impact on the business creates accountability. Asking every day, "How can we do things better?" must be part of the job description.

Employees don't trust managers who don't care about their safety, working conditions, pay, job security, etc. Managers, on the other hand, don't trust employees to do their best work and care about the business when they do the bare minimum, don't show up at all, produce and accept poor quality, etc. It is a chicken-and-egg scenario, where the chicken definitely comes first. If leadership invests in its people and treats them well, the employees will respond. Those who don't must be let go. It starts and stops with leadership.

Sustainability transforms the corporation from a mere mechanical organization into an engaged team.

This section emphasizes that the sustainability of continuous improvement requires putting the safety and other needs of employees first and then asking them to hit new and more demanding targets. Given that basis, employees must be held accountable to sustain the newly implemented processes and help the corporation grow and succeed.

Sustainability is all about preserving the beautiful new processes and positive culture that came out of the implementation phase. If a new culture, one that values engagement, responsibility, teamwork, high standards, mutual respect, and commitment, is not sustained, old ways and old processes will creep back in.

When the CEO, top leaders, managers, and employees sustain a commitment to the never-ending journey of continuous improvement, they create a legacy that will keep generating ROI for the corporation, the employees, and the communities around them.

105

Without trust within the corporation, there can be no #Sustainability. Employees work just to hit the daily goals. They don't think about changing for the better.

_____

_____

_____

106

CEOs must be willing to: 1) change employee performance plans and 2) ensure that the newly implemented process becomes the standard of work. These two things will guarantee #Sustainability of #ContinuousImprovement.

_____

_____

_____

107

One organizational readiness survey showed that 70% of corporations did not maintain their standard of work. There's no #Sustainability if employees don't follow a certain standard.

108

The newly implemented ideas should become the new standard of work. Otherwise, employees will just go back to their old ways. #Sustainability

---

109

Every process needs to have a standard of work to ensure that the game of the team is #Sustained. This will prevent bad quality from seeping back into the process.

_____

_____

_____

110

Every process should have proper documentation so it can become the new standard of work. #Sustainability

_____

_____

_____

111

When processes are documented, operational knowledge is preserved. It can be used to 1) improve the current state and 2) reduce training costs in the future. #Sustainability

_____

_____

_____

112

In #Sustainability, what gets measured gets improved. Measure the performance of your team to see if the new standard of work is being sustained.

_____

_____

_____

113

When the standard of work is #Sustained:
1) quality mistakes can be avoided,
and 2) employees stay accountable to not
change the process.

_____

_____

_____

114

It's all about the culture first. It's about the processes
second, and it's about #Sustainability through our
people. —Parker Hannifin on M.A.R.I.S.

_____

_____

_____

115

When #ContinuousImprovement is not part of the employee performance plan, their focus is only on reaching the targets. They won't care whether they contribute to cost reduction and process improvement. #Sustainability

_____

_____

_____

116

How employees are rewarded for their daily or annual performance is what drives personal behaviors. #Sustainability

_____

_____

_____

117

If CEOs want #ContinuousImprovement in the DNA of their corporation, they must change employee performance plans. Number 1: safety; number 2: on-time and complete delivery; number 3: quality; and number 4: cost reduction. #Sustainability

_____

_____

_____

118

Putting the employees first means talking about their safety before asking if the corporation won or lost yesterday. #Sustainability

_____

_____

_____

119

Change the DNA of the org so it's focused on employees first. This will drive the behavior that CEOs want from their employees while still getting the margins they're looking for. #Sustainability

_____

_____

_____

120

When CEOs focus on the safety of their employees first, they are showing up front that they care about their people. That engages employees right off the bat every day. #Sustainability

_____

_____

_____

121

Everybody in the org is a key player. Managers wouldn't want to lose anybody, which is why safety should be number one. #Mobilization

_____

_____

_____

122

The Hawthorne Effect for the positive happens when there is trust and #ContinuousImprovement in the corporation. The effect is creating positive changes without anybody actually asking for it. #Sustainability

_____

_____

_____

123

Trust, in the context of #ContinuousImprovement, works two ways: 1) employees are accountable about their performance plans, and 2) CEOs trust their employees to implement their ideas.

_____

_____

_____

124

#Sustainability of #ContinuousImprovement creates an environment of trust. When trust exists from top to bottom, CEOs and managers can focus on greater things for the benefit of the corporation.

_____

_____

_____

125

If a culture of trust is created in the corporation, employees will feel comfortable to do what they know is right. This will empower them to deliver more than what's asked from them — more than what the CEOs think they need. #Sustainability

_____

_____

_____

126

When trust is imprinted in the corporation's DNA, it results in a collaborative capability to create #ContinuousImprovement. This will get the corporation to a whole new level of engagement. #Sustainability

_____

_____

_____

127

The ultimate output of #Sustainability is an environment of trust and collaboration. This empowers the corporation to #ContinuouslyImprove even without the CEO being physically there.

_____

_____

_____

#ContinuousImprovement solves the issue of sustainability once and for all. It empowers the employees to take ownership of the process in such a way that they eliminate waste on a daily basis.

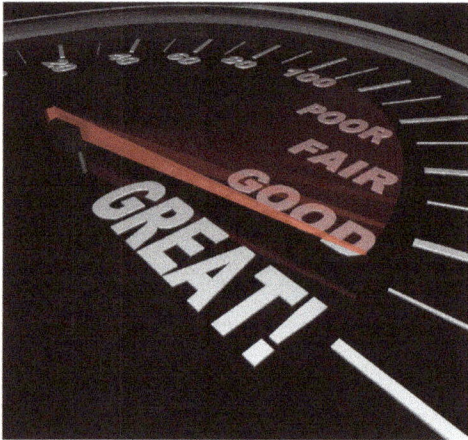

John Ballis
https://aha.pub/RapidROI

Share the AHA messages from this book socially by going to
https://aha.pub/RapidROI.

Scan the QR code or use this link to watch the section videos and more on this section topic:
https://aha.pub/RapidROISVs

Section VIII

Conclusion

We've seen companies that refused to continually improve and went out of business. Hungrier and more nimble new competitors with higher quality, lower costs, better designs, and better service took business from them. Some refused to innovate or change and became obsolete, while those with continuous improvement in their DNA stood above the rest.

While much of the focus of continuous improvement is on empowering employees to eliminate waste and improve quality in their daily operations, it is equally valuable up the chain of command. Better decision making, problem solving, reporting processes, and information gathering can all be improved every day, just like line operations. Corporations that embrace CI by whatever name they call it enjoy high satisfaction ratings from customers, better sales, and more profits that can be used for better pay-outs to investors, better pay for employees, more R&D, and more advertising and sales efforts. Then, the cycle repeats. Better paid, empowered, and treated employees, from the board room to the shop floor, are engaged to deliver the best quality in everything they do. In all the great cultures that we've named, everyone has a sense of ownership and cares about the company's success win. It's not complicated. It's just hard. But isn't excellence always this way? Ultimately, it is the CEO who decides culture. Companies and cultures are, in large measure, reflections of leadership.

128

The clock is ticking for corporations without #ContinuousImprovement set in place. Whether they like it or not, they will lose in an aggressively evolving competition if they don't change.

_____

_____

_____

129

A #ContinuousImprovement journey benefits not only the present state of the corporation but also its future. It's a never-ending cycle of making the corporation better than it was before.

_____

_____

_____

130

Corporations that have embedded
#ContinuousImprovement in their DNA will stand above
the rest because they have empowered their employees
to operate with zero waste daily.

_____

_____

_____

131

#ContinuousImprovement drives employees to believe
in what is possible in the corporation.

_____

_____

_____

132

With #ContinuousImprovement, the CEO will recognize that sustainability comes through an engaged culture. This is the kind of culture that provides on-time and complete delivery to customers every day.

_____

_____

_____

133

With #ContinuousImprovement, employees work every day on a process that they own. They easily see the value-add and non-value-add in it. They clearly understand the cost of operating the business.

_____

_____

_____

134

#ContinuousImprovement creates employee engagement at a level where they can identify how to eliminate seconds, minutes, hours, and days in the process. That means reduced cost and a better EBITDA.

_____

_____

_____

135

Employees have a sense of ownership of the corporation's success when they are geared toward #ContinuousImprovement. This sense of ownership makes them want to sustain what they started.

_____

_____

_____

136

#ContinuousImprovement solves the issue of sustainability once and for all. It empowers the employees to take ownership of the process in such a way that they eliminate waste on a daily basis.

_____

_____

_____

137

CEOs would want the ability to transfer knowledge so it becomes part of the corporation's DNA. This will enable the corporation to sustain its #ContinuousImprovement journey.

_____

_____

_____

138

Every CEO wants to leave a legacy as their footprint in the corporation. A journey of #ContinuousImprovement could be that legacy.

_____

_____

_____

139

Every CEO wants the corporation to continually grow and prosper well beyond their years of being physically there. #ContinuousImprovement makes this achievable.

_____

_____

_____

140

When a CEO succeeds in setting up their corporation on a #ContinuousImprovement journey, they can look back and say, "I started a legacy that never ends."

_____

_____

_____

A Little History on Lean — The Rest of the Story of How M.A.R.I.S. Came About

Toyota begins its journey and sets the stage for what world-class continuous improvement looks like.

Throughout history, business professionals have admired successful companies as role models for continuous improvement. One of the greatest is Toyota, the famed Japanese automobile manufacturer. However, most people don't understand how or why Toyota began continuous improvement.

In 1950, Toyota set off on a journey of continuous improvement for many different reasons. The company had a high defect rate per car and a long cycle time with high manufacturing costs. They were losing $1,600 per car sold in the USA. The transformation that made Toyota a great and profitable company—one that has become the benchmark of transformation for factories and created the standard in the industry—is valuable to serve as an example of how much change is both possible and necessary to make a company great.

The story behind their original name and why they had to change it is also interesting. Their journey serves as an example of radical transformation: since Toyota began the continuous improvement approach, they have gone 360 degrees from the point where they started. Just as Toyota shifted their methodologies, resulting in a complete transformation of their culture and practices, so this book fundamentally shifts the way we view continuous improvement, operational excellence, and Lean transformation.

When reading about Toyota's journey, recognize that its success is not a formula to follow. Its story primarily serves as an example of the potential to change a work environment, as well as a cautionary tale about how much effort and commitment is necessary for this type of metamorphosis to happen.

Toyota's journey to success is intertwined with the story of continuous improvement philosophies and methods. In the past fifty years, there has been not only a transformation in Toyota but also a complete alteration in the philosophy of continuous improvement.

The graph on the next page shows the manufacturing revolution since the 1950s, which has embraced numerous continuous improvement methodologies, which, under many different titles, have become the new conventional wisdom about continuous improvement.

Though business professionals tend to think in terms of half a century for the development of continuous improvement, prior to the 1950s, Frederick Taylor set up

Continuous Improvement has come 360 in 50 years

Application Philosophies and Methods

As early as 1950s, Toyota started a continuous improvement process and called TPS in the late 70s. Key influencers to this process were Dr. Deming, Dr. Shingo and Henry Ford manufacturing process after World War II.

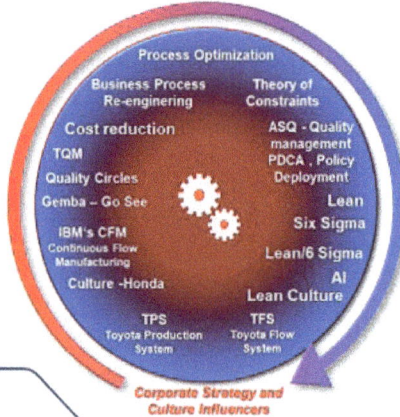

Process Optimization

Business Process Re-enginering
Theory of Constraints

Cost reduction
ASQ - Quality management
TQM
PDCA , Policy Deployment
Quality Circles
Gemba – Go See
Lean
Six Sigma
IBM's CFM
Continuous Flow Manufacturing
Lean/6 Sigma
AI
Culture -Honda
Lean Culture

TPS
Toyota Production System
TFS
Toyota Flow System

Corporate Strategy and Culture Influencers

From a focus on quality circles to as late as Lean – Six Sigma driven by colleges/academia world. The concepts of continuous improvement have taken on many different names through the years. Fundamentally two things came out of Japan, one from Toyota on process improvements and second one from Honda on culture of engagement.

a gospel of continuous improvement and motion studies designed to reduce waste. According to Taylor, every process has a flow. There's not a single thing we do as human beings that cannot be present on a flowchart or a value stream map. The flowcharts identify the steps to complete tasks in every aspect of our life.

Since Taylor, we have embraced almost every methodology and philosophy for studying time and motion, sometimes without enough evaluation or analysis. Most of these philosophies have come from academia. Ever since Toyota began its successful continuous improvement processes, many methods for this approach have emerged. From a focus on quality circles to Lean/Six Sigma, continuous improvement has been driven by academia, which does not always transfer successfully into the corporate world.

However, as the author of *Good to Great*, Jim Collins, stated, "We don't have great schools, principally because we have good schools. We don't have a great government, principally as we have good government. Few people attain great, in large part because it is so easy to settle for a good life. The vast majority of companies never become great, precisely because the vast majority become quite good—and that is their main problem."

There is a need to step back and assess the relative value of each of these methodologies and distinguish which ones are simply good and which ones are the most valuable and can potentially lead to corporate greatness.

As early as the 1950s, Toyota started a continuous improvement process that came to be called "TPS" (Toyota Production System). It has remained an integral part of Toyota's commitment to excellence. Toyota is a great company because it does not settle for just being good; in fact, it has never claimed to be world-class. The company understands that its journey of continuous improvement is a lifetime journey of eliminating waste. No one will find Toyota jumping on the bandwagon of "latest and greatest" theoretical philosophies or culture change in any "program of the month."

While other companies settle for quick-fix solutions, gimmicks, and poorly thought-out recommendations, Toyota focuses on developing a long-term strategy implemented in its daily culture to eliminate waste. Any organization looking for future success should do the same on a daily basis. As at Toyota, the ultimate goal of a company should attempt long-term sustainability.

While much change is necessary to correct the pathways that many companies have taken, this book does not ask corporate leaders to start over. It is important to build upon what you have started but also to become aware of the organic needs of your organization and to meet those needs with the best methods of becoming a Lean enterprise. This book helps you understand why 96 percent of all transformations in companies fail, whether these transformations include becoming Lean through initiating operational excellence programs, Six Sigma, or any other domain of continuous improvement.

This book also reports data from a survey completed in Fortune 1000 companies. The data reveals the real reasons that continuous improvement at most companies is not sustainable. Perhaps most importantly, the discussion of futuristic Lean is not an academic exercise. Consequently, this rethinking is not academic or theoretical. This book is about how companies can create their own journey based on the company's DNA, which makes them unique. It takes readers through the historic journey of Toyota becoming a leader in the industry through continuous improvement. Toyota, like many other companies, initially started by having many different consultants assist it in rebuilding its manufacturing. The book lays out a transformational process that can be tailored to your company and work. However, we focus on the necessity of originality, discuss ways to discover corporate uniqueness, and evaluate its role in successful corporate transformation.

As we begin, it's important to ask: why have so many companies tried to emulate successful companies, such as Toyota, Motorola, IBM, or others of the 4 percent? There exists a notion that success can simply be copied and that a cookie-cutter approach when designing a strategy for sustainability will yield a successful result. This idea is more wishful thinking than reality, but it is an oft-adopted method among company leaders.

I do not recommend giving business professionals a cookie-cutter approach to design a strategy for sustainability. Rather, M.A.R.I.S. attempts to get corporate leadership to understand that Lean transformation must be developed to be compatible with the DNA of the individual company. It must be symbiotic with its vision, values, and long-term strategy. The latter must also be sustainable over management changes—it should transcend the individuals who implement and design it. Furthermore, the strategy has to be sustainable through the ups and downs of the market and ultimately, through leadership changes at the C level of a corporate organization. This kind of strategy builds the company toward greatness.

Toyota: The journey begins

After World War II, Japan was attempting to rebuild its social structure and economy. The Emperor Hirohito was no longer considered a deity, and the war machine was dismantled. In the midst of these monumental changes, Toyota tried to re-establish itself, though the original name of the company has a historic context that helps us understand the change from the family name to what we recognize today.

The founding ancestor of what became a legendary corporation, Sakichi Toyoda was born in Japan in 1867. A hard-working businessman, he built a small company that manufactured textile looms.

When Toyota started building cars, Toyota chose to run a contest to change its name from Toyoda to Toyota. But why? A likely reason is that the family name was well known in Japan and had controversial associations. When I was working for IBM, we studied the Japanese methods and methodologies at Toyota. In 1987, we were told that the name change came about because of Soemu Toyoda, an admiral in the Imperial Japanese Navy. Associations with this military leader would have been controversial because he did not follow the conventional thought about the war. He carried a reputation for being difficult to work with and opposed attacking the United States. This opposition and his preference for naval power rather than the army probably resulted in his demotion from the Supreme War Council and his reassignment to command the Yokosuka Naval District.

Toyoda later assumed command of the Imperial fleet in May of 1944 and devised risky strategies for the Imperial navy during some key battles where Japan was defeated. Because the navy was already vulnerable due to fuel shortages, he risked a battle that was unlikely to bring victory. After the atomic bombs on Hiroshima and Nagasaki, he opposed the surrender of Japan, arguing for defending the island nation and fighting to the last man.

After the war, Soemu Toyoda was tried for war crimes but acquitted. He was the only Japanese military leader charged with war crimes to be acquitted of the charges, and he was released from prison in 1949. These associations would have been present in using the name "Toyoda" for the automobile manufacturing company name and probably contributed in part to the name change.

Soemu Toyoda

By understanding the public's concern about the name and seeking publicity through an advertising strategy, the management and owners decided to let the public participate in a logo design of the company to rename itself. Thus, the name of the company changed from Toyoda to Toyota. I believe that this was the start of Toyota's transformational journey.

Toyota, as we know it today, is identified as a leader in continuous improvement. Its methods and philosophies are known and admired throughout the world. The recognition is justified based on what it has achieved throughout its transformation. Though most businesspeople would consider Toyota world-class, the Toyota team simply believes that their transformational journey continues today just as it did in the beginning. In other words, they do not rest on their laurels, nor do they let their phenomenal success become an excuse to cease continued effort at improvement. Let's examine why they believe that their journey continues the same way today.

Over the years, Toyota has been continually refining all its processes, including all the manufacturing and business processes. In some ways, Toyota's methods come from and reflect Japanese culture, which emphasizes a long and rigorous practice in order to become a master of any traditional art or ritual. For example, it is not unusual for a person learning the tea ceremony (a highly refined traditional ritual in Japan) to study with a master teacher for fifteen to twenty years. Acquisition of mastery in any task is not truncated or hurried, and there is a different understanding of how much practice and effort must occur before excellence is achieved. In the corporate culture of Toyota, this understanding of a long timeline has been incorporated and applied to the improvement of all its workflow processes.

I've had a tagline for many years: every process has a flow and it can be improved. I learned this from the Japanese. Toyota did not become a master of improvement overnight; it took years for it to become renowned as one of the best companies in the world. Though corporate America borrows a cultural value of efficiency, which has produced many good results, especially in the automation of design, it's important to recognize when efficiency fights against mastery in business processes and becomes an enemy of greatness because not enough time is allocated to identify where to improve a process. Also, efficiency may be a reason that the process is not revisited once improvement has been made, resulting in "good" but not "great" processes.

Taiichi Ohno, a Japanese industrial engineer, was heavily involved in what became the concept of the Toyota Production System. In the early days of transforming Toyota, the management recruited Shigeo Shingo from Mitsubishi, another automobile company. Shingo was revered as one of the best in creating cycles of time improvements through many of his concepts, and he had an eye for seeing non-value-added waste in processes. Dr. W. Edwards Deming was also hired, to focus on quality improvements. He was revered as one of the worldwide experts in quality from the USA, most notably in SMED (single minute exchange of dies).

While these men helped initiate significant change at the company, Ohno became concerned about manufacturing processes and quality efforts reverting to old ways due to cultural behaviors. His metaphor for this relapse was "the grass growing back." He created the concept of standard work to prevent the company from returning to previous manufacturing methods. Toyota created the TPS as a way to continually improve its operations in order to reduce costs and increase sales.

For an example of Toyota's dedication to the improvement journey, we can study an engine plant that reduced cycle time from eight weeks to fewer than eight hours. While this represents an extreme reduction of time and the ultimate in manufacturing efficiency, this plant completed more than 250,000 kaizen events over fifty years to achieve this performance.

Kaizen refers to what most people know as a team's change event, meant to continually improve their operation by engaging the employees to participate. Many books focus on kaizens in companies; however, like many things that have come to America, they have been misunderstood and misused. In the old Japanese language, "kaizen" simply means, "what good looks like." It is the key driver of the TPS.

In the beginning, the word was used when abnormalities were observed through the measurement system within Toyota. When a process had a repeated failure, managers would put together a kaizen team made up of engineers, managers, and employees to quickly solve the problem. The team would collect data, sometimes for weeks, on their communication control board before acting.

Think of these communication boards or centers as like monitoring the core information needed for patients in critical care. The visual management centers are divided into three key sections for hourly and daily operational metrics. The far left of the board starts off each day with people, with safety as the number-one concern. The middle of the board monitors the performance of the processes for a given area. Quality delivery and cost are the three critical metrics that are non-negotiable, though a team can add more key performance metrics. The right section of the board is for continuous improvement. All concerns about the previous hour or day are captured to ensure employee engagement.

The visual management board was critical in the advancement of the TPS. Within Toyota, it became a critical factor for ensuring continuous improvement, with the team leader having conversations with their fellow team members to understand where the failures and opportunities were within their process. They would track these failures as opportunities in a Pareto diagram to be matched up with the area's value stream map.

Toyota has applied continuous improvement to all areas of its business, including working with suppliers for higher quality and just-in-time deliveries of all kinds of inventory. Continuous improvement has been the catalyst for its growth and its journey from good to great. Though Toyota is admired in the world as a great company, it has taken over fifty years for it to reach the milestone that it's at today. The company looks at waste as the enemy. It has a basic metaphor of not capturing the enemy but eliminating it to ensure the company's competitiveness throughout the world. However, it's important to understand that they do not look at people as waste. Total quality improvement is an opportunity to identify the root causes of failure and refine or remake the process to allow people to produce the best quality within that process.

Lean Your Way Creates the Foundation: What Do You Expect on the Journey to a Lean Transformation?

Explanations for the high failure rate of continuous improvement programs include lack of leadership, an unengaged culture, and incorrectly applied or weak methodologies. However, from my observations in the continuous improvement sector for over thirty years, I would say that one of the most critical success factors is whether there is a clear communication plan for the journey. It is also important to recognize and knock down the myths about what is going on within companies on their operational excellence journey, in order to help support anyone on their own journey. Some myths that have been created by consulting firms and the academic world need to be abandoned on the journey; they are counterproductive and can hurt a company's progress in transformation. I believe that most companies in the "other" 96 percent are not failures by industry definition. To begin to gauge the reality of your company's condition, I hope that as you read, you open up your thought process to ask questions about where your company is and what you believe is occurring within it. This discussion will support your reflective process and share information to facilitate deeper analysis.

Which set of fish do you want to swim with? Review the graphic below and think about how much influence comes from simply swimming with the school and relying on that instead of thinking through issues that will give you insights to take you from good to great.

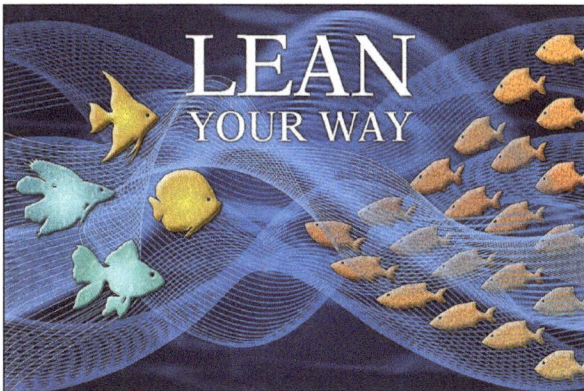

I've seen many companies embark on an intended Lean transformation, setting out with big ambitions and high expectations. A huge initial effort gets the project off the ground, enormous excitement arises as to the possibilities that Lean offers for the business, and a hunger for success is pervasive. But over time, the enthusiasm ebbs away. All those good intentions gather dust in the back of a cupboard. In spite of the initial enthusiasm, it is extremely important to remember that the top four companies viewed as successful practitioners in the world of Lean did not get there overnight nor did their success come from a magic formula. Why do you think that the industry has seen a 96 percent failure rate associated with Lean transformations? Several key factors contribute.

1. There's a deferment of ownership of the process of becoming Lean.

In the beginning, companies need specialists who have not only certifications but also sufficient experience implementing Lean transformations so they can identify when to apply the correct tool. Organizations also need a specialist who can communicate the vision through the application of continuous tools.

However, achieving a Lean transformation is not about having a handful of specialists or a department dedicated to the journey. A Lean transformation enables everyone within the organization to acquire the basic skills to identify any problem that inhibits the ability to meet a customer's expectations. Everyone is on the journey, not just the specialists. In this sense, a Lean transformation is very much a "do it yourself "project—a company can only be assured that the work that must occur to become Lean succeeds if those within the company do that work.

At Toyota, employees not only learn metrics on an hourly or daily basis, but they also learn how to see with their own eyes when waste and abnormalities occur in the work process. Toyota has refined its process for employees, so they engage immediately. The workers can identify the root cause of a problem and implement solutions. Ownership of the process is a fundamental necessity for Lean transformations to work, and deferment of ownership, whether given to specialists or "delegated" to lower levels of management because executives are "too busy," is the first step on a path to transformation failure.

2. Companies falsely believe in and try to practice a cookie-cutter approach to Lean transformation.

It's easy to believe that the achievement of Toyota or another of the 4 percent successful companies can become the pathway for others to follow; however, each company maintains its own processes, and many of these are not analogous to any other organization. Using the "cookie-cutter" approach cuts off vital aspects of processes indigenous to the organization, which weakens rather than transforms it.

Leaders who attempt a "one size fits all "approach to Lean transformation in these organizations confuse the ultimate goal of efficiency in their company processes with the ongoing, sometimes tedious, procedures of refining steps that can make that goal a reality. In this case, leaders observe the end product of a successful journey. They then try to bypass the long and arduous trek by simply copying what another company has done. These individuals have confused reading postcards from the journey for the excellence of taking the trip themselves. The trip can never be repeated; it is individual, requiring time and effort. The journey does not work as a vicarious experience. Each company has its own map to draw as it explores making Lean changes to the work environment.

For Toyota, the journey began over fifty years ago and contained many bumps in the road and patches of rough terrain. As an example, the engine plant named after Shingo focused on eliminating non-value-added activities in their processes. When they began, the procedure to change the manufacturing environment from being able to produce a 4-cylinder engine to a 6-cylinder engine took weeks. Shingo introduced the concept of SMED (single minute exchange of dies). The weeks turned into eight hours. However, this transformation was not magical; it didn't happen with the flip of a switch or the click of a mouse. It took over 350,000 kaizen events to achieve. As a leader, do you believe that you have the courage and stamina to remain on the journey regardless of how many continuous improvement events it may take? An enduring commitment to your company's unique journey, not a flirtation with a new technique, is mandatory for a successful Lean transformation.

3. Another key factor contributing to failure is organizational changeover.

Because the journey requires time and endures beyond any C-level leadership, there must be a "cultural DNA" that protects the journey, commits to the Lean transformation process, and transcends change even at the C level. A company culture that sustains Lean transformation and provides support for ongoing refinement in the manufacturing or business processes is not a celebrity culture based upon the personality of a single individual. Though the DNA is influenced by leadership at the highest level, there is no genetic determinism that prevents the company from transcending leadership change. The journey continues even when one captain is replaced by another on the long voyage. This "cultural DNA" is deeply embedded: Toyota built its DNA to always ensure that culture was engaged from leadership throughout the company.

Considering the three factors that contribute to failure, what do you believe it will take for your company to be part of the 4 percent, versus the 96 percent that never seems to reach greatness? Similarly, are you willing to make the quest for greatness an ongoing journey? Did you know Toyota does not consider themselves world-class because they believe that there is still opportunity every day to eliminate waste in their processes? Toyota believes that once you claim that you are world-class, you will likely slip backward into the 96 percent because you will become complacent with the status quo.

If companies that are focused on continuous improvement can avoid the pitfalls that many companies encounter during their journey toward a Lean transformation, they can be part of the 4 percent. I believe this because I've been in the industry for over thirty years and have completed over 100 Lean transformations in just about every sector of business. I know there are four areas where companies systemically fail during their Lean transformation. If a company can avoid or resolve the issues around these four areas, it can become great.

Part of my assurance about success comes from a completed survey of Fortune 500 companies with 10,000 participants at all levels. This research confirmed the following: all four categories are linked together because the first category is foundational, with the following three categories depending upon it. It is based on the root cause of all transformation failures: poor communication. Overall, being unable to continue a journey involves a lack of true commitment from leadership, company boards, and owners of businesses, which is reflected in poor communication and the problems that can ensue.

1. Communication is the root of all failure.
2. False-starts to continuous improvement transformation are a significant pitfall.
3. Lack of organizational alignment of personal performance plans from the top down breeds failure.
4. No organizational readiness for 100-percent culture engagement means a failed endeavor.

As we look through the diagram, it becomes easy to understand how failures happen so frequently. If 87 percent of the people in the organization are confused or unsure of what their roles are in bringing about the transformation, then it is logical for failure to occur. During any organizational change, there is a certain level of anxiety among workers due to the new expectations and the human desire to avoid risks that might bring failure. Most people do not intentionally want to fail at their occupation; however, in a transitional time, if roles have not been communicated clearly, then the fear is sufficient to bring about resistance to any change because the risk is assessed as severe, so there is little motivation to act in new ways.

When leaders communicate the roles and expectations that they have for the people in their companies in the transformational process, it feels less risky, and employees are more likely to engage in the changes. For this to happen, however, the leaders must have a clear sense of direction; they must know in which direction to proceed and be able to communicate that to all stakeholders. A review of each linked reason shows that communication has failed sufficiently to undermine any possibility of success.

Additionally, the data implies that the lack of communication arises from a misunderstanding of the nature of Lean transformation and the amount of effort required to enact it. There must be a shift in understanding that avoids a gimmicky approach to the process. If leadership has only a short-term perspective, the transformational processes will probably become false starts. While certain improvements in work processes can happen quickly, making deep changes (as we learned from Toyota's example) requires months and sometimes years to develop.

What Causes Failure?

1. Communications: PDCA Your Role Out?

Let me share a scenario that I have often seen from my work with companies.

Someone from the leadership, such as the CEO, goes to see a facility that claims to be Lean by every measure. This executive is completely wowed by the tour (a charged-up tour team can usually leave visitors wowed by the results). The team tells the visiting executive that they are doing 5S. The visitor sees a place for everything and everything in its place. They are impressed by the pull system of the flow of the product and the information displayed, as well as the "visual management" depicting a high degree of control, which results in excellent on-time delivery with low levels of quality defects and rework. Furthermore, they see a workforce that is engaged within the facility. Every employee can be approached and is working with a high degree of control and confidence—almost like a stress-free environment. In addition, the facility is doing this with surprisingly old and unimpressive equipment. The visiting CEO is totally sold on this "Lean journey, which might become the program of the month."

Upon returning to their home company, the executive promptly gathers the rest of the C-suite and with conviction and passion, declares that this "Lean" is "exactly what we need." With animation never before displayed, the CEO relays all the wonderful things that they have just seen. Soon, they are surrounded by a group of disciples and followers. Everyone devises a plan by appointing a Lean Leader. This person is a mid-level manager who is proficient in many of the required techniques and has been a vocal advocate of Lean for years. Next, they appoint a core team to work with the Leader—the Lean implementation team—and announce that the Leader will unveil the Lean implementation plan in thirty days. The team publishes the implementation plan for the management team on schedule. They want to get everyone involved, so their year-one objectives are to implement 5S and standardize work across the company.

Next, the Lean, or Operational Excellence, Leader and their team start teaching the rest of the company. The Leader and the team not only introduce the initiative but also share the tools. They are then required to follow up and assist the various locations as the workers implement the Lean tools.

This sounds like a good plan, right? Don't be fooled. According to the CEOs, when the transformation process is left to the lower level of management, there is a high level of failure. In my survey analysis, 83 percent of companies failed to transform when the above scenario happened.

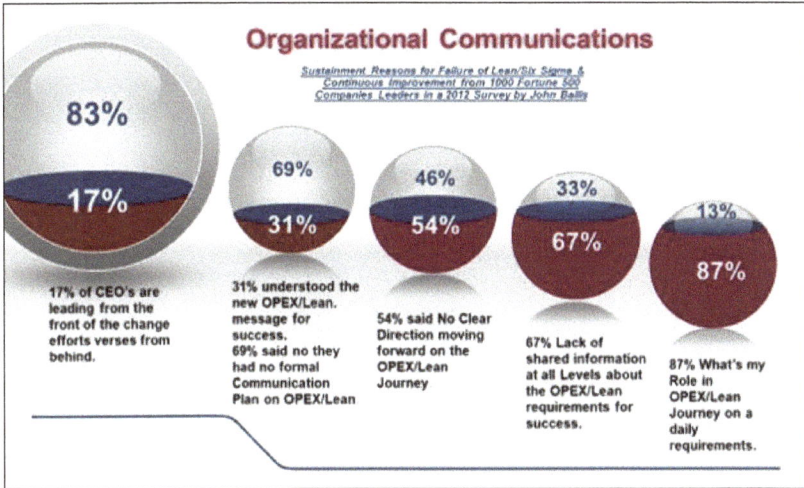

Organizational Communications

Sustainment Reasons for Failure of Lean/Six Sigma & Continuous Improvement from 1000 Fortune 500 Companies Leaders in a 2012 Survey by John Bailly

83%
17%

17% of CEO's are leading from the front of the change efforts verses from behind.

69%
31%

31% understood the new OPEX/Lean. message for success. 69% said no they had no formal Communication Plan on OPEX/Lean

46%
54%

54% said No Clear Direction moving forward on the OPEX/Lean Journey

33%
67%

67% Lack of shared information at all Levels about the OPEX/Lean requirements for success.

13%
87%

87% What's my Role in OPEX/Lean Journey on a daily requirements.

Everyone understands how busy the C-suite is when running the business. However, what I have found through this survey is that only 17 percent of CEOs actually lead a company transformation from the front; 83 percent of CEOs lead from behind. However, most of the companies that created a successful Lean transformation assigned the CFO or the COO to lead the journey.

Because the transformation includes all dimensions of the business, it is important that those with authority and vision captain the voyage to Lean transformation. When a midlevel manager becomes the change agent, the situation is like hiring a trainer to get fit, but the trainer then assigns you a new trainee who is trying to become a trainer but has no authority at the peer level to create change. The CEOs whom I have interviewed believe that this is a critical failure on the part of most CEOs because they do not understand what value their presence will ultimately create. They don't understand the need for the executives to create belief in the journey. In the transformation, it is imperative that engagement, rather than delegation, happens at the C level.

Former CEO Don Washkewicz of Parker Hannifin said, "The number-one fatal Lean implementation error is the failure by CEOs to invest adequate time in change management and communication tools. These tools ensure the implementation achieved is a culture transformation, which is a vital prerequisite to the successful application of any change initiative." The ownership of this kind of change needs to arise from the top level of the corporation, and that level must believe in the change enough to invest time and effort to see the company become a different entity.

As an aside, it is important for those leading the organization to reflect honestly about their own attitudes toward change—not as a rhetorical device to spur motivation and appear dynamic, but as something that will also demand changes in methods and focus. In Lean transformation, everyone is affected, and each has a role to play to bring success.

As an example of a company that corrected its problems, the Dr. Pepper Snapple Group had multiple false starts due to communications. When the senior management team came together for a week-long strategy workshop, one whole day was committed to communication. Even though the corporate communication officer was part of the team, they designed a rollout of the critical success factors associated with a good communication plan. Understanding that the senior executives could not be at every kickoff, they produced a video of commitment. Each senior leader participated in a ten-minute video that all employees would see during announcement week. To ensure all 12,000 employees had access, they posted this video on a private YouTube company site. At every kickoff or kaizen event, the video would be played to assure every employee once again of the management's commitment. Furthermore, most members of the C-suite actually rolled up their sleeves and assisted in the implementation at a kaizen event. Modeling expected behaviors by leadership is powerful in the change process; it demonstrates direction and commitment that speaks louder than words.

Secondly, there was a conference call set up so a member of the C-suite would participate in every report out of a kaizen event. Later, we will discuss successful requirements to replicate Dr. Pepper's incredible results. Marty Ellen, the CFO of Dr. Pepper, was the leader of the continuous improvement journey. Marty came from Snap-on Tools, with a deep belief in continuous improvement/Lean from that company's deployment. He uniquely came up with a title for the journey: rapid continuous improvement (RCI).

"John played the lead role in the design of our lean transformation. His design of super kaizen's that brought dramatic results in eight weeks or less contributed to the $175 million reductions that Dr. Pepper Snapple Group promise Wall Street. His ability to engage the organization is what makes him uniquely different from other lean practitioners."

Marty Ellen
Former CFO of Dr. Pepper Snapple Group

He not only communicated their commitment to all employees but also made a commitment to the stock market to reduce costs by $150 million within three years. A robust communication plan was the key.

To further understand why communications are so important and why a weak communication plan leads to failure, the survey revealed that 69 percent of companies said that they had no formal communication plan. Only 31 percent of the companies surveyed were given credit for having a plan. However, even within this 31 percent, a mixed mash of communication plans was not always designed to be successful. Some failed to ensure that the rumor mill would not create a deluge of negative thoughts about the journey. There were no weekly newsletters, videos of events, or clear messages of results. Management teams would often hide the financial results for overt reasons of information protectionism; however, those putting forth the added effort required in this type of change needed to know that the extra work and stress involved in the change was making a difference.

A successful company in a transformation is transparent to ensure that employees develop a perspective that the trustworthiness of the journey is real. Privately held companies seemed to do a better job of overall communications and transparency than corporate entities in the survey. Results drive enthusiasm and ensure commitment to the journey.

The survey also revealed that 54 percent of companies had no clear direction moving forward. Here's a scenario that happens in most companies. Leadership finds an area—one that I would call cherry-picking—to ensure success. There's nothing intrinsically wrong with this. However, if you don't have a clear way of replicating the process that got the results, then you're more likely to fail the next time. It is critical to have a strategy and a project plan for how to move forward to secure success, which must include how you will select the people who will

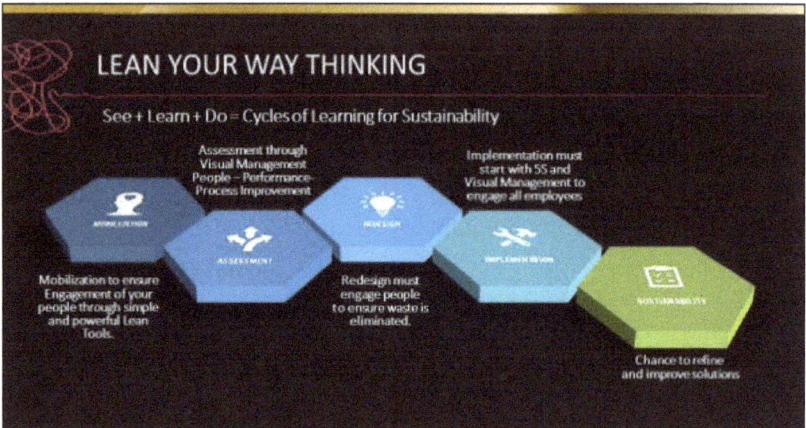

be deploying the training and implementation, as well as a budget—regardless of the results from the initial selection of projects—to be implemented through kaizen events or other mechanisms.

The strategies must also include an implementation execution methodology that is easily understood and can be enacted consistently throughout the journey. This is the company's path forward and must include a vision of the continuous improvement operating system for success.

At a quality conference, I had an opportunity to go head-to-head with Michael Hammer, who co-wrote the book, *Reengineering America*. I challenged Michael to tell me what his project steps were that a team would follow. I recited from his book and asked him about step 178. He danced around the question for several minutes. The fact was, he did not remember what his execution methodology entailed.

A forward-looking journey must have a simple execution methodology. The methodology I have been using for more than thirty years is simple, though it has matured into five phases and fifteen steps. We will cover these in detail later, but below is a simple graph that takes you through the phases.

- Phase 1: Mobilization—full organizational engagement from top to bottom and bottom to top
- Phase 2: Assessment—full understanding of the value streams from an enterprise level and value stream maps in every department to identify waste

- Phase 3: Redesign—rapid improvement tools for rapid results
- Phase 4: Implementation—ownership by employees to ensure engagement and get results faster
- Phase 5: Sustainability—required monitoring through auditing weekly, monthly, quarterly, and yearly—change all performance plans for all employees regardless of level in the company

This execution methodology is a patented change management practice called M.A.R.I.S. It was developed in 1992 and has remained successful in helping companies through their Lean transformations. Coupled with this methodology is the Deming philosophy: Plan-Do-Control-Act (PDCA). M.A.R.I.S.'s execution methodology and PDCA are part of an insurance policy for consistency of execution. This was the driving force behind the Parker Hannifin corporate-wide, worldwide transformation of Lean through their program called Targets. This was the start of my journey developing a methodology that could be used to ensure the execution of Lean transformations and to keep it simple.

#2. False Starts

Approximately 67 percent of companies said that there was a "lack of shared information at all levels about the OPEX/Lean requirements for success." Therefore, employees are being asked to participate in the transformation without understanding the requirements for success. Many are given high-level improvement tools with little detailed training on how to deploy those tools. In addition, management fails to allow the time required for teams to be successful. Many reasons for false starts are related to the leadership's commitment; many employees tagged these events as just another program. Eighty-nine percent of these companies reported false starts due to a lack of organizational readiness to step up to the plate—it simply did not exist. Ninety-four percent of companies surveyed said that their employee performance plans did not align. At the end of each year, 90 percent of all company employees were on some type of performance plan.

For a Lean transformation to work, when employees face evaluation and are rewarded for their performance for the previous year, managers must ensure that the performance plan requires employees to be part of the continuous improvement effort. Basically, performance objectives need to be related to the transformation and have been spelled out to hold people accountable. The result of not including this in the performance plan of employees means the journey becomes the program of the month. Of those surveyed, 89 percent of company employees said, "This will pass like every other cuckoo idea that senior leadership comes up with to make us help improve their bonuses."

At Toyota, continuous improvement is the second requirement on every employee's performance plan. The first requirement is to be safe. To avoid the pitfall of false starts, once again, leadership must think through the strategy and understand what needs to be communicated and changed to ensure success at the end of the day. People are motivated by money and to a certain extent, security in a job. If that performance plan does not relate to what employers are asking employees to do on a daily, weekly, and monthly basis, the continuous improvement journey will fail. In this situation, whatever improvement happens will be short-term and short lived. For example, if my supervisor tells me to get a raise, I must complete 100 widgets at 100 percent quality and on time, then I have a goal. However, if the boss tells me that I need to complete 100 widgets at 90 percent quality and that I'm going to be given time to work on a team to improve upon the other 10 percent, I am more likely to participate as a team member.

It's important to think through what we're asking of employees: to commit to the release of their creative ideas to reduce costs with their engagement. Accountability comes through personal performance plans specifying what's required of an employee. Once I had a CEO change all the performance plans across an entire corporation. He started with himself and had four criteria on his plan:

- Each day, I must come in and review safety to ensure that I have a safe environment for all my employees as my number-one responsibility as a leader.
- Cycle time reduction to deliver on time.
- Cycle time reduction to improve quality.
- Cycle time reduction of everything I do to reduce cost daily.

He said, "If I reduce cycle time, the quality of our product will be delightful to our customers. If I reduce cycle time, my on-time delivery and commitments to my customers will be met. If I reduce cycle time, I'm reducing the cost of doing business and creating shareholder value."

To create a simple understanding of what was required, he eliminated a 360-page employee review manual and reduced it to one page. In this large corporation, after mobilizing and assessing the HR functions, they redesigned functions to a simple format and implemented it corporate-wide. The simplicity had great resistance from HR, but it saved $12.6 million annually in the review process of employees.

To ensure that false starts are eliminated, leadership must have alignments within the organization and organizational readiness. Until this is displayed in a value stream map of swim lanes, management does not understand the cost associated with reviewing employees annually. The details for each employee uniquely link to the operation they perform, whether for a piece of equipment, service, delivery, back office, or front office. Furthermore, there should be no difference whether someone is on the floor or at the top level. Every employee should be consciously aware of safety and the consequences from a quality, delivery, and cost standpoint. Employees need alignment to ensure that the long-term strategy is achieved to become a Lean transformation company.

#3. Organizational Engagement Alignment

In reference to organizational engagement, 67 percent of employees surveyed believed that they either had lost power or were limited in their involvement. Many organizations get caught up in this scenario because they either hire "master black belts" or train their people to be green belts. In this process, only a select few receive training, and the vertical structure solidifies so workers do not feel empowered to contribute to the transformation. The transformation gets sidelined by organizational politics related to status. Too many organizations allow their companies to be hijacked by those who have been certified with these titles. Unfortunately, many of the people leading these engagements or projects do not meet the requirements by the organizations that have certified them.

Know that certification for doing projects does not automatically translate into making a good coach. Can you imagine what would happen if you put your child in a car and gave them driving lessons and then turned the keys over to them? What a disaster that could be. To ensure organizational engagement, all employees must participate in the company, the department, and/or the function they belong to as a team member of continuous improvement.

Going back to false-start solutions, if you want to secure employees' engagement, then put specific requirements into their performance plan. This ensures employee engagement because of alignment to the journey. I'm not suggesting that leaders must spoon-feed their employees: these individuals are mature adults and should understand the job requirements based on the company's philosophy of continuous improvement. But this is not subject to whether they want to participate. I can't tell you how many times I have seen the resistant employee on a team eventually come up with a great idea to reduce cycle time and improve the process.

Organizational alignment only happens through servant leadership at all levels. It is successful by creating an environment of accountability for everyone to ensure the sustainability of the journey. This means a leader or manager might have to change the work environment to create centers that allow innovation and creative thinking to occur. For some leaders, this means modifying the need to feel in control of all aspects of the business, including employee behavior. A paternalistic attitude toward subordinates is not helpful for this kind of transformation. In fact, this feeling of control is an illusion, anyway, because people are free agents. But it is important to remember that given a reasonable set of guidelines and sufficient support (such as training) to change, most employees will sign on for the journey.

Not all companies can create a work environment like Google. But any organization can create small environments and training rooms that stimulate creative thinking. Dr. Pepper created an organizational license for continuous improvement, calling it a "kaizen license" to operate on a continuous improvement team. The license came with the fundamentals and philosophies to guarantee consistency of learning throughout the organization. It also gave the person the right to participate in a team after successfully going through a super kaizen event of training that took over eight weeks.

During these eight weeks, we created one consistent way of mapping, which was visual and inspired people to eliminate waste. We also created one consistent communication center that focused on safety quality cost, delivery, and continuous improvement. Such consistent engagement supported employees through simple methods and procedures. Organizational engagement is critical to the success of any Lean journey, which is a transformation of the company. By the last week, which was implementation week, employees had successfully been trained in the basics of Lean/Six Sigma.

#4. Resistance by Employees

The survey revealed that in 98 percent of the companies that attempted a Lean transformation, there was a fear of the unknown at every level. Fear saps the energy needed to bring about a Lean transformation, and it is the primary cause of resistance among employees to organizational change. Without clear communications, avoidance of false starts, and employee engagement, leadership will always find resistance by employees. This is even truer in union facilities, governmental operations, and health organizations—basically, in 98 percent of all companies. The resistance created by fearful employees often takes the transformational journey and reduces it to programs of the month.

In a company during any change, there will always be 10 percent of the people who resist. Then, 80 percent of the people will go along with the flow, and 10 percent will excel at making changes and enjoy the environment of continuous improvement within a company. The primary resistance comes from employees who believe that this is a mechanism for rightsizing an organization. These individuals see the change as a threat to their job security. While it is true that sometimes there are unknown market factors that will lead to an organizational downsizing because it must have the right size based on economic reasons, but this is not a given in Lean transformation, and it is important to share this information with employees. In any case, clear communications help dispel organizational resistance.

If there are no economic reasons to reduce the number of employees, then let natural workforce reductions be your friend. This means that sometimes, employers might have to carry extra people on the payroll. When Lean initiatives or a Lean transformation is associated with rightsizing and results in the potential for downsizing, it is a death spiral that the company's initiative will never come out of. The rumor mill will run rampant throughout the organization, and people will begin to say, "I told you so; this was a downsizing exercise." The backroom conversations and negativity will run amok and derail the journey.

Commitment to "Lean Your Way" must flow from the bottom levels up to the top. Top leadership must lead from the front through a set of principles. They must put the principles into action, and only then can they motivate and guide their teams by example. Management must make these principles a way of life. The CEO may feel that continuous improvement is the responsibility of a manager and a select few leads by a master black belt, but this is leadership by exemption rather than example and weakens the potential for success.

Continuous improvement leaders should have thorough knowledge about the Lean methodology and build up confidence among followers. Some organizations that also fail as a core team of belt holders consider this to be just a part-time job. However, the leadership needs to concentrate full time on the areas of improvement linked to the vision of the organization; otherwise, the strategy falls right down.

The organization should select the best people for the team, those who are future leaders, and groom them to be in future management roles. Otherwise, the journey is a splash in the pan and management has mud on their faces. The investment is lost because the short-term view wins out versus the commitment to stay on the path that may take years, like Toyota's journey.

About the Author

John Ballis

In this book, John Ballis shows how to avoid failure with a simple execution methodology. You will learn how to apply Lean, Continuous Improvement daily by engaging how your organization operates with a powerful process to eliminate waste. He has coached in more than 2,000 kaizens and 100 Super kaizens and worked with over 100 companies to create their Lean Transformation. He specializes in assisting leaders to increase profits while bringing Rapid ROI into every aspect of their Lean journey.

AHAthat®

THiNKaha has created AHAthat for you to share content from this book.

- ➲ Share each AHA message socially: **https://aha.pub/RapidROI**
- ➲ Share additional content: **https://AHAthat.com**
- ➲ Info on authoring: **https://AHAthat.com/Author**

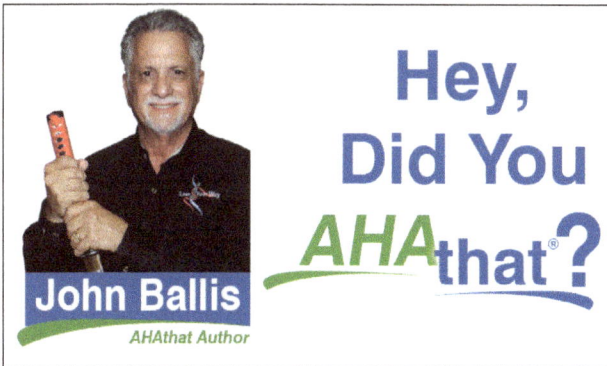

Hey,
Did You
AHAthat®?

John Ballis
AHAthat Author